The Tree on the Bluff

c.l. mcmanus

© Copyright 2025
First Edition 2025
All rights reserved.
Published in the United States
ISBN #978-1-7358997-2-5 (paperback)

Some names and identifying details have been changed
and/or combined to protect their privacy

To Kim and Joan,
who gave me the time and
understanding I needed,
free from judgement

And ~ To all the
other trees, reaching
their roots to find
solid ground

CONTENTS

Prologue
1

Part I – Insight

****

Poem 1 – **The Tree on a Bluff**
"Insight is born in the tree on a bluff"
5

Poem 2 - **Learning to Live**
"Reciprocal judgments are futile"
11

Poem 3 - **This Fellow Man**
"One set of circumstances away
from self-destructive behavior"
17

Poem 4 - **The Curse of Indifference**
"Hard lessons learned as awareness awakes"
23

Poem 5 – **Unmarked Trails**
"Risk is in the safety of the common and mundane"
29

Part II – An Awareness of Experience

****

Poem 6 – **When No One Was Looking**
"(I) took in my surroundings
minus self-conscious regard"
35

Poem 7 – **The Source**
"Friend against friend disregard and offend"
41

Poem 8 – **A Brief Hesitation**
"I questioned my own faith (and) hated
thinking that I'd gone there"
45

Poem 9 - **Lone Goose**
"Empathy does not lie"
51

Poem 10 – **The Ripple Effect**
"The beauty in lifting the burden,
of suffering alone"
57

Part III – Self-Compassion

****

Poem 11 – **When**
"When did the arrogant soul
leave its humble beginning"
63

Poem 12 - **Peacefully Alone**
"They, haven't walked in our shoes"
67

Poem 13 – **Broken becomes Whole**
"Respite is insight sleeping in the soul"
73

Poem 14 – **Valuable**
"At long last a sense of worth awakes"
77

Poem 15 – **The Fifth Season**
"I've matured slowly, but perhaps "deeper"
than someone having the cocoon of both
parents for a good deal of their life"
83

Part IV – Acceptance

****

Poem 16 – **Unforgiven**
"Mercy can be given but not taken"
89

Poem 17 – **From this Day Forward**
"From this day forward now has new
meaning, one I will accept"
93

Poem 18 – **The Whisper**
"I saw them whisper; I wish I hadn't"
97

Poem 19 – **Surrendering**
"A life out of hand, only He can wield"
103

Poem 20 – **Destiny's Light**
"All along He had me where
I knew I should have been"
109

Part V – Gratitude

****

Poem 21 – A Valued Friendship
"So few can accept, or understand,
but my friend stood by my side"
115

Poem 22 – Charming Ol' Gal
"A striking round door, brass slot for the mail"
119

Poem 23 – Time Well-Served
"Our four-legged friends are gifts undeserved,
a gift of perfection, and time well-served"
123

Poem 24 – Tom
"Making the best of life, with grace"
127

Poem 25 – A Lifted Soul
"Poetry lifts the soul and floats beyond,
where continuous thoughts lie still below"
131

Part VI – Humor

****

Poem 26 – **May-September**
"The man who took a chance"
139

Poem 27 – **A Gifted Memory**
"Deer in the headlight moments"
145

Poem 28 – **Growing Pains**
"Middle school is a rite of passage"
151

Poem 29 – **Chickens and Roosters**
"Women don't change much, even as they get older"
157

Poem 30 – **Splendor**
"But she let out a toot, like an underwater flute"
163

Epilogue
167

About the Author
169

Prologue

Poetry is "writing that formulates a concentrated imaginative ***awareness of experience*** in language chosen and arranged to create a specific emotional response through meaning, sound, and rhythm," at least according to the Merriam-Webster dictionary. Amongst a methodical definition were three words: Awareness of Experience, that captured, for me, an overlooked word: poetry. Poetry seemed the one tool that could capture, validate, and release overwhelming feelings in a beautiful yet seemingly fragmented world. Anything that can lighten the load of everyday struggles should be shared.

After exhausting conversations regarding life's difficulties with almost anyone who crossed my path, I realized vast support exists with years of philosophers and ordinary people, past and present. They empathize through their words and wisdom; it's nothing less than invaluable. The truth is, the answers are all there, and we stumble on them all the time.

> "I will love the light
> for it shows me the way,
> yet I will endure the darkness
> because it shows me the stars."
> – "Og" Mandino, author (1923-1996)

Mandino's calming words resonated with me, as did countless other words from many different people. I've tried for years to understand my weaknesses and internal battles, as well as our strange world.

My survival techniques have been far-reaching, from innocent enough humor to not-so-innocent numbing with alcohol, to calming words. Thank God for calming words, compassionately finding their way to us. The poems herein and their related stories are my own words from my own walk. These words represent thoughts and struggles, determination, and resolve. They are a quiet awareness of experience. The photos contained within (exc. cover) are also my own, symbolizing a significant freeze-frame moment that spoke to me with understanding and gratitude. My thoughts, stories, and poetry are interspersed with wisdom from others, in quotes, that helped get me through personal trials and experiences. I hope they, in their entirety, resonate with you as well…

PART I
Insight

one

The Tree on the Bluff

Insight is born in the tree on the bluff
That reaches its roots to find
Balance that only the tree on firm ground
From the onset had been assigned

Resolute small roots scream out in silence
Only briefly stopping to rest
To gather their purpose for pressing on
A seemingly deliberate test

Trials and reflection, unrelenting
And yet, water to its roots
Finding their way to solid ground
And well-earned attributes

It's a thing of beauty, those gnarled veins
Absorbing the stress of life
To help the tree grasp on and upwards
Forgetting the emptiness behind

*Insight is born in the tree on the bluff
That reaches its roots to find*

After sorting photos from a vacation in and around Athabasca Falls, Alberta, Canada, I noticed a remarkable symbol of resiliency. A tree grew in the upper left corner of a snapshot of the falls, growing out of a rock bluff. At the base of its gnarled trunk were sprouted roots that were, at first glance, anything but pretty. They grew in sharp contrast to the perfect water rushing below, water that sliced through molded layers of rock accented with healthy greenery. The contrast seemed that of those with a seemingly easy path versus the unending challenges of others. Nonetheless, the roots personified strength and determination wherein they stretched into thin air on a journey of purpose, regardless of hardship.

Struggles and their resulting strength and drive are a thing of beauty, joined with something spiritual. Though I grew up attending church every Sunday, I've never considered myself very religious. If anything, for a long time, I've resented the obligatory nature of organized religion and bitterly looked for what I *didn't* like about it. One such excuse came my way on the heels of my chaotic late teens after attempting to talk to a church priest regarding ongoing struggles. My attempt at counsel ran head-on into a dangerously insensitive church secretary. She quickly put the kibosh on my request by announcing, "You can't just walk in here; he doesn't have time for you!" The result was more self-loathing and a decade-long church hiatus. It wasn't until the maternal tug of marriage and children that the notion of exploring faith again felt sincere.

I'm by no means staunch. Other than raising an eyebrow, I hold no extreme judgments against differing opinions. After speaking with a priest (this time, I got in) about my restless search and unending questions, he replied with sincere and supportive compassion, "I just don't think you're there yet." He said other things, alarmingly spot on (meaning I had two raised eyebrows and an open mouth), but his approach and words, "(not) there yet," were comforting. This is my path.

Besides looking up, so to speak, it's been various authors, speakers, friends, and family that initiate "ah-ha" moments. Reading from others about similar struggles, especially in the latter portion of my life, slowed my hyper-sensitive focus on judgy "firm ground trees." And even within Hollywood movies, wisdom is nestled despite their sometimes cringy material. The pages following sporadically cite these improbable sources of insight ~ *City Slickers* raises the topic of what's truly important, and *The Quiet Man* is a wholesome story from another time. *My Cousin Vinny* embodies much-needed humor and a validating dose of humility, and *The Money Pit* normalized marital stress. With the help from both likely and unlikely sources, "I'm straining toward what is ahead."

> "Brothers and sisters, I do not consider myself yet to have taken hold of it. But one thing I do: Forgetting what is behind and straining toward what is ahead." - Philippians 3:13

two

Learning to Live

A life of charm veils the perception
Leading the blessed to take exception
Haven't walked in our shoes
They believe what they choose
Never needing the wrong direction

Learning to live without their approval
Turning a leaf instead is crucial
Must be a lesson
Nevertheless in
Reciprocal judgments are futile

If there's one thing in my life, I've found hard to accept, it's judgmental people with an advantageous edge. Be it a solid emotional grounding or a remarkable support system, they flippantly condemn those without the same who sometimes go in the wrong direction. I could feel only contempt for them, and that resentment kept me from looking inward for a long time. It was innate knee-jerk behavior to zero in on their dismissive actions rather than to accept that their views are formed from their experiences, not mine. I need not make everyone think as I do, and it was toxic to try. Accepting offhand remarks didn't validate their comments but merely acknowledged that they were clearly coming from a different place.

Weaning myself from focusing on those with dissimilar experiences and veering 180 degrees, embracing those with similar ones, brought gratitude. Their words became my understanding; mercifully, I wasn't alone. As long as I'm wholeheartedly honest with myself, I'm qualified to do my own validation with the help of supportive words, writing, and wisdom. They're everywhere.

Shared words came my way through an online post from Mindsjournal.com, "I want someone I can share my entire life with, who will leave me alone most of the time." And to that person(s), I say thank you for your words of familiarity.

Actor and comedian Darrell Hammond said, "Learn to forgive yourself for the things you did in order to survive." The nudge was welcome; forgiving yourself is okay if future intentions are honorable.

Author and motivational speaker Zig Ziglar said, "There will always be people in your life who treat you wrong. Be sure to thank them for making you strong." Fair enough.

I've often taken the wrong road. I've spoken when I should have been silent and screamed when self-control ought to have been practiced. I've taken on responsibilities I had no right to and injured myself and others in the process. I've followed the lies of false acceptance. I've trudged through periods wherein I was emotionally unavailable to others. When the hurt maxed out, I was willing to try anything, eventually looking inward. Carl Jung said, "Everything that irritates us about others can lead us to an understanding of ourselves." I often had to ask myself, "why care what any one person does, thinks, or says." However, truths about myself *would* subsequently come to light. With it came a new awareness that, with the help of lessons learned from others, helped me to start walking down a new road.

three   *This Fellow Man*

I saw the man who trudged alone
his youthful soul was gone
The public passed him on the street
but dare not look upon
For if they looked with any depth
they might find out that he
This brother, son ~ this fellow man
is just like family

I saw the gal who lay alone
as the crowd lingered round
To watch the fountains rise and fall
at the Bellagio, they found
A like-minded acceptance
to pretend that they don't see
This sister, daughter ~ worthy soul
is just like family

The tightness of a family bond
a magical connection
So rarely seeks to go beyond
its walls and risk infection
But let us not forget
the lonely and dejected
Someday, somewhere, somehow,
we may be the ones rejected

While walking along a busy street in Seattle, I encountered a young man who looked to be in his early twenties. He appeared to be on drugs and trudged along, wearing a surrendered blank stare. His pants were soiled with diarrhea, and though he seemed oblivious, he had perhaps a tinge of awareness of what he had become. He wasn't much older than my own son, and the cold disregard of the massive crowd walking by was disturbing. It still is decades later.

> "Before you pass judgment on one who is self-destructing, it's important to remember they usually aren't trying to destroy themselves.
> They're trying to destroy something inside that doesn't belong."
> -JmStorm, author and poet

My husband and I were in Las Vegas when, as par for the course, we walked to the Bellagio hotel for the water fountain show and display. Amongst a massive crowd of vibrant tourists was a person lying on the concrete sidewalk, covered by a blanket. No one, including us, checked on this person's condition. We quietly remarked to one another, "That guy could be dead for all we know." Honestly, we had no idea if the person was male or female. The empathy was fleeting, tucked away, but not entirely forgotten. It's easy to take brief pity and then separate ourselves from the unrecognizable world of the ill-fated. However, we'd be remiss to say we aren't all one set of circumstances away from self-destructive behavior, even on the level of the stories herein.

The phrase "just like family" is a sticky wicket. Although the two stories included are extremes, and it certainly is human nature to feel compassion and inclusion on some level, unfortunately, it's also human nature to distance oneself from people who don't fit in. Be it the ruthless effects of drug abuse or a homeless drifter at the one extreme, or simply an awkward soul at the lesser, if you're the one on the outs, it feels merciless.

> "The most terrible poverty is loneliness,
> and the feeling of being unloved."
> - Mother Teresa

four

The Curse of Indifference

What if our time could roll in reverse
Mistakes that were made no longer a curse
Perfection perfected
And lessons unlessoned
Arriving not having rehearsed

Life is a classroom within the mistakes
Hard lessons learned as awareness awakes
Connection is lost
If teachings are tossed
And indifference then overtakes

The discouraging moments of my life replay in my mind often. "I wish I'd known at the time," or "If only I'd tried harder to be..." It's exhausting, nonetheless I'm confident it helps to keep me humble and empathetic. They say you're not supposed to let regrets run your life. But it's difficult not to ruminate painful lessons, and in a manner of speaking, regrets *should* run your life in the way of guidance. Regrets help identify that one thing you need to stick to ~

In the movie *City Slickers*, Mitch, a discontented urbanite played by Billy Crystal, attends a modern-day cattle drive with two of his good friends. Each man faces challenges as they approach middle age. One of the guides for the cattle drive, Curly (Jack Palance), plays a no-nonsense cowboy who offers no-nonsense advice and turns his attention to Mitch:

Curly: Do you know what the secret of life is?

Mitch: No, what?

Curly: This (holding up one finger)

Mitch: Your finger?

Curly: One thing, just one thing. You stick to that, and everything else don't mean sh*t.

Mitch: That's great, but what's the one thing?

Curly: That's what you gotta figure out.

Unequivocally, that one thing for me has been to recognize when I've taken on more than I can handle and reverse course when appropriate. But the memories are mine to keep, for better or worse. Upon seeing others "lose it," my seasoned empathy is alive and well; I've been there. If time could roll in reverse, we'd have the opportunity to avoid the mistakes, losing the grief they caused. That very pain gives us the gift of empathy, hopefully keeping us humble and from being indifferent to others.

> "There's nothing harder than
> the softness of indifference"
> - Clare Boothe Luce, author (1903-1987)

five

Unmarked Trails

Take an adventure on an unmarked trail
Unforeseen insight will quickly unveil
Adversity brings strength
And time will ascertain
Risk is in the safety of the common and mundane

After working in my "degree" field for 25 years, primarily sitting behind a computer, I took a considerable risk and opened a small retail store. My knowledge of operating a small business was next to zero. Proceeding with what could only be described as a burning desire for adventure and independence meant facing the fear of social situations and the very real fear of failure. However, the near decade-long experience was unknowingly "exposure therapy," as overcoming social anxiety became par for the course, and failure, at least as a whole, would not overwhelm my adventure.

My personal unmarked trail has tallied well over 20 jobs over the years; it's bordering on embarrassing. However, it's given me an awareness not found on the more standard, "marked" trail. I've learned first-hand, from various positions, that many things cannot be read about in a book but rather felt through a range of emotions. Arguably, the one job that gifted me the greatest lesson in kindness, through experiencing marginalization, was working fast food. I remember all too well the looks from those who thought of us employees as somehow "less than," ranging from customers to management. Largely because of that experience, I'll forever be particularly respectful to anyone working in the service industry.

Working as a cashier as a 16-year-old, and then again in retirement, taught me that standing at a register for eight hours as a 16-year-old is vastly easier than doing so as a 60-year-old. It's given me a newfound empathy for anyone in that position, "not by choice." But it was much more than that. I was quickly aging out of a fast-paced technology-driven world, one no longer wanting traditional ways, traditional values, or us baby boomers. It wasn't fun. A touching scene from the TV show *The Gilmore Girls* (season 2, episode 12) depicts the father of the main character (Richard and Lorelai, respectively) attempting to live a new life as a middle-aged retired man. Subsequently feeling unwanted by those closest to him, including his own daughter, remarks to his daughter, "Suddenly, I realize what it feels like to be obsolete. I hope that you never have to learn what that feels like."

My 25-year-long career in land surveying, floating in and out of many similar workplaces, showed me a range of values and humor. I couldn't have gotten the priceless visuals, memories, or lessons without the experience of "same job, different place" over and over again. My decision to job-hop within my field, and outside of it, has no regrets, though it certainly isn't for everyone. After deciding to leave my "field," opening my own small retail store, I learned that I could overcome most any fear relatively quickly. The unmarked, squirrely trail gifted me with unforeseen insight, adversity, strength, and, ultimately, understanding. Yes, I felt stupid sometimes, but I ultimately gained confidence with a sense of accomplishment through facing my fears.

> "Two roads diverged in a wood and I – I took the one less traveled by, and that has made all the difference."
> - Rober Frost, poet

PART II
(an awareness of) Experience

six

When No One Was Looking

*When no one was looking
I bent down on one knee
to examine the work
from a spiders' long eve*

*The web she had spun
hung heavy with dew
showcasing its' strength and
daily artwork debut*

*When no one was looking
I let down my guard
and took in my surroundings
minus self-conscious regard*

*I did one last surveillance
before following the norm
when no one is looking
there's no need to perform*

The web she had spun hung heavy with dew ~

Stop and smell the proverbial rose, even if you are self-conscious. Practice mindfulness; take photos of nature and frame them. Notice the spider webs, and if you're lucky enough, witness one as it's spun. If you're painfully insecure, or even if you're not, do it when no one is looking; silence enhances everything. Much of what we need to practice self-kindness has been given to us through the perfect artwork, sounds, and scents in nature.

I've ultimately embraced my oftentimes-distant self, a personal trait not exactly celebrated in this world. So, I was joyful and validated upon happening on a kindred spirit of sorts while visiting the homestead of Josie Bassett Morris in the Northeastern corner of Utah. A plaque in her honor read in part: "This cabin and the nearby structures are part of the homestead established by Josie Bassett Morris in the early 1900s. Nearing 40 years of age, divorced and with her children grown, Josie wanted a home of her own. She chose this spot for its plentiful water and good pasture, the natural resources necessary to grow fruits and vegetables and raise cattle. Braided rugs softened the cabin floors, handmade quilts warmed the beds, and Josie's favorite pictures hung on wallpapered walls. In summer, beds of cosmos, marigolds and poppies ringed the cabin. Family and friends from Vernal (Utah) often visited. There was always lots of work and never much money, but life at Cub Creek suited Josie's independent spirit. She lived in this cabin until shortly before her death in 1964 at age 90."

Somehow, I could see myself blowing out the evening candles, snuggling under several quilts, and going to sleep to the sounds of crickets, and my cattle grunting as they readjusted and dropped down for the night.

*Standing by the cabin of my "kindred spirit"
Josie Bassett Morris, Utah*

seven

The Source

Social platforms and embellished clickbait
A malevolent plan to decimate
Friend against friend
Disregard and offend
Partaking like fools in evil debate

Like-minded thoughts gathering force
Wicked intentions controlling the course
Unfriending creates
A harem of mates
Who never give thought to the source

Achieving a peace in turning away
Distantly watching the games that they play
A calm disposition
Without your permission
Can never be taken away

Look no further than divisive social media posts to witness dark human behavior through malicious words and the narcissistic need to be right. Author Richard Carlson expertly said, "Have you ever noticed that practically everything you read justifies and reinforces your own opinions and views on life?" He explains ditto heads, who egregiously think, "I already agree with everything you say. Tell me more." Although I generally follow the no-divisive posts rule on social media, viewing them and their cascading comments captivate me. I'm intrigued by how people genuinely do surround themselves with ditto heads, mingled with very few opponents. Social media has provided a boxing ring of sorts with words in the ring, spectators in the stands, and hearts pounding with aggression. Against my better judgment, I've "engaged" once or twice where I was NOT a ditto head. Though braced for a kickback, I misjudged. The Facebook junkies interlaced their fingers, cracked their knuckles, and let me have it. Too clear is the memory of *intense* self-inflicted pressure to participate in battle. My heart raced; it was an awful feeling. We're here to learn, in part through unceasing triggers. With effort, I've learned to begin resisting provoking encounters or adding fuel to the fire. Malevolence surrounds us, and there's peace in the simple act of acknowledging it instead of engaging in battle.

> "Seeing into darkness is clarity. Knowing how to yield is strength." – from Chapter 52 in the Tao Te Ching

eight

A Brief Hesitation

*Attacks on religion cleverly veiled
Ultimate goal the faithful derailed
A brief hesitation
Subtle motivation
As seeds of doubt prevailed*

*Watching friends and family lose faith
Like-minded thoughts allow them to feel safe
Arrogant and proud
No divergence allowed
In the hopes of a brief hesitation*

Subtle suggestions give way to subtle hesitations. Jokes about religion can be funny, but there's an underlying message if it's truly disproportionate. Like so many other things, social media has stoked the fire. I questioned my own faith when a shard of doubt flashed through my mind. Rejecting the feeling, I hated thinking that I'd gone there. Life's suffering from current and past world events causes doubt; it's unquestionably disturbing. It isn't normal not to ask, "Why?" But agonizing on where to pin absolute blame is a death spiral to faith. Accepting that we don't know everything gives us a solid footing to start the more commonsense approach of what we can do to make a positive difference. And after reading the soothing words, "lean not on your own understanding," within Proverbs 3:5-6, it all but stopped the spiral and put forth the words that strengthened my faith. I wouldn't lose myself debating cynics who thrive on condescending division. When feeling lost in an increasingly confusing world, I could find peace knowing that perhaps we were never meant to understand everything fully. It IS the basis of faith. I don't have all the exact answers; no one does.

Years ago, my husband did a solo seven-day hike in the Olympic National Park, Washington State. We both started camping in tents in our early twenties. We saw firsthand how youthful invincibility brings the advantage of seeing things you probably won't see later in life because you probably wouldn't do it. During this lone hike/camping trip, my husband got turned around on the maze of trails after not seeing anyone for days. He began to talk to himself for some time before he literally asked aloud, "God, I wish there was somebody around to ask." Just then, he heard a "hello" from behind. Startled, he spun around to see a middle-aged gentleman, a bit heavyset, wearing a t-shirt and a very small day-pack. After briefly discussing potential trails, the gentleman said, "Oh, you needed to take the left-hand trail; you need to backtrack." My husband plainly states, "That interaction stayed with me a lifetime; I'm convinced he was my guardian angel." The pessimists would say there's no proof in that. No, there isn't, but there have been numerous times throughout my life that I've been stopped in my tracks with "whoa" moments; most everyone has. You have two choices: cynicism or faith; I choose faith. And not because it's easier; it's definitely not easier.

In *The Book of Joy,* the Dalai Lama says, "There is a Tibetan prayer, which is part of the mind-training teachings. A Tibetan master says, 'Whenever I see someone, may I never feel superior.'" I state my position from time to time, but hopefully without arrogance. I can only communicate what I've "felt" from experiences, reading, prayers, and reflection. My belief is that God is everywhere, and He helps to teach us in His way and in His good time.

nine

Lone Goose

*I heard his call before I saw
the lone goose in the sky
A fellow soul who tugged upon
my sympathy just by*

*The way the sound that should have been
accompanied by others
Harmonized with beating wings
o'er the ground he covers*

*And when he landed on the lake
the others swam away
I felt the awkward tension
of the lone goose kept at bay*

*It seems we had these things in common
empathy does not lie
I recognized and shared the feelings
of the reclusive lone goose cry*

I heard his call before I saw, the lone goose in the sky ~

I enjoy alone time, probably too much, yet fear being excluded. So, mixed feelings were very real while attending my first silent retreat for four days and three nights. Initially, there was an eagerness to experience the calm that silence would bring. I anticipated safety in breaking from the norm of having to fit in, watching words and avoiding potential judgments that lurk in everyday conversations. At the same time, shaking the discomfort of leaving the familiarity of the norm or risking something worse in the unknown was difficult. Regardless, I walked into the room of 28 strangers, sat down, and searched their faces. They were likely seeking the same thing I was: a connection to something outside the frivolous nature of putting on airs through social media and of living in a disturbingly fast-paced, very loud, and confusing culture. After a welcome lunch, we were directed to respect each other's wish for near silence. It wasn't easy for some, but painfully easy for others. Our retreat leader spoke intermittently throughout the next few days, leading us in prayer and offering thoughts on which to reflect. With no TVs or computers, our cell phones lay, silenced by choice but there as a lifeline to familiarity. In between gatherings, we were free to walk the beautiful grounds where deer grazed in relatively close proximity. An unusual number of flowering shrubs mushroomed along walkways, attracting diligent bees and graceful butterflies. Views of the Mississippi River and the sounds of water being pushed from barges fighting their way upstream or floating downstream were rhythmic. And the silence from human voices enhanced everything.

Paths through the woods walked solo were eerily unfamiliar and yet beautiful. Light streamed through the branches like spiritual artwork, almost as if on cue. And, of course, we were free to retreat to our private rooms to "just be" in quiet separateness. The solitude, or rather fear of it, gripped me only once while walking down a long, empty hallway toward my room. My fear was that of being permanently cursed with the aloneness sought. Like the lone goose calling out, I didn't want to be alone, not really. At the closure of the retreat, several participants offered telling facts. For some, this was their twentieth or thirtieth silent retreat. It was comforting to know that others shared my longing for partial solitude. If you've ever closed your eyes while taking a deep breath, and let it out slowly and purposefully, you know the release of tension. The silence was like that but a hundred times the intensity.

Lastly, one summer, I had the privilege of working at a local golf course. My duties included, in part, driving a beverage cart on the course alongside joyful patrons. Amongst a backdrop of sculptured fairways edged with trees and grassy roughs, were ponds, wildlife, and winding paths that interspersed it all like a yellow brick road to OZ. With little time to take in my surroundings when it was busy, a picturesque landscape awaited when it wasn't. I'd soak up the solitude peppered with the occasional "tink" of a golf ball while sitting in awe of the Disney-like backdrop. Squirrels, rabbits, deer, and the occasional turtle making his way across a dew-covered fairway before the day got underway is the world behind the noise. It's an overlooked gift of healing.

I'll never know why that goose was alone. Perhaps he'd lost his mate, had been shunned, or was in a temporary separation; one can only assume it wasn't by choice. However, the rare sound of lone beating wings in tandem with a solo call was captivating. I've gambled with relationships by requesting "to be left alone," risking rejection, and quite honestly, receiving rejection from time to time. I don't want to be lonely; I just want to be alone from time to time; it can be beautiful.

> "Being alone for a while is dangerous. It's addicting. Once you see how peaceful it is, you don't want to deal with people anymore." -Tom Hardy, Actor

ten

The Ripple Effect

Taking in joy, witnessing empathy
Through a strangers' display of caring
Who feel the hurt of another then share
In the burden of pain weight-bearing

Then light the torches of others to see
The beauty in lifting the burden, of
Suffering alone, that's why it's so clear
The ripple effect to ease hurting

While watching the TV documentary (*Mission: Joy, Finding Happiness in Troubled Times*) centered around a meeting between the Dalai Lama and Archbishop Desmond Tutu, I was gripped by one visual in particular. Video captured the two men as they listened intently to a young girl's heart-wrenching story of losing her family at a young age. Her pain was unmistakable. Immediately following, the Dalai Lama spoke to the girl, providing sympathetic and validating words stemming from and centered around strength and hope.

The archbishop waited patiently to address the child while wearing a pained look of empathy during the young girl's testimony. Watching the archbishop listen to the young girls' story while wearing a genuine look of distressed sympathy made me feel physically achy, and I had to ask myself why it hit me so hard. The answer came later when the archbishop was asked, "How can we achieve Joy and Happiness?" He answered, "Joy is the reward, really, of seeking to give joy to others. When you are caring, compassionate, more concerned about the welfare of others than of your own, you suddenly feel a warm glow in your heart because you have, in fact, wiped the tears from the eyes of another." The feeling of a warm glow in my heart came in the form of an ache, and it was *hope* from simply witnessing sincere compassion from one human being for another. It was hope that people truly could care for one another, weakening the daily news propaganda that there is no hope. It was a ripple effect from a stranger's example of caring.

"Recent research by social scientists Nicholas Christakis and James Fowler suggests that this ripple effect (from kindness and compassion) can extend out to two and three degrees of separation. In other words, experiments with large numbers of people show that if you are kind and compassionate, your friends, your friends' friends, and even your friends' friends' friends are more likely to become kind and compassionate."

-from the book *The Book of Joy*,
His Holiness the Dalai Lama,
Archbishop Desmond Tutu & Douglas Abrams

PART III
Self-Compassion

eleven

When

*Crossing paths with people whose arrogance
Undermines feelings and brings unbalance
When did the arrogant soul
Leave its humble beginning
Armed with boldness, obsessed with winning*

*Calming myself, I begin to protect
A cut so familiar, I often neglect
To take a deep breath
And slowly release the
chaos and noise, to find my inner peace*

It is hard to believe that we're all born, by and large, the same. It was Albert Einstein that said, "The only thing more dangerous than ignorance is arrogance." At what point do some assume the role of arrogant aggressor, or its belittled polar opposite, hypersensitive defender, while a fortunate few adapt and calmly sit back?

When ultimately recognizing and accepting that some delighted in my thin skin, I was empowered and knew exactly what could be taken back. I clearly could not engage in heated conversations, and in any case, it was foolish to do so. I wised up, slowly removing myself from triggers and welcoming the possibility of a new, laid-back temperament.

> "One of the best lessons you can learn in life
> is to master how to remain calm.
> Calm is a super power."
> -Bruce Lee, martial artist, actor, philosopher

twelve

Peacefully Alone

Desperate attempts to try and be heard
Toning down efforts as the mind matured
Trusting in yourself
In lieu of persuading
Brings calm instead through mind and soul training

Eyes closed while breathing deeply on a beach
Barefoot in the sand, warm water within reach
Peacefully alone in tranquility
Balanced in absolute humility
Judgement of others gone, the love of God upon

*Eyes closed while breathing deeply on a beach
Barefoot in the sand, warm water within reach ~*

They, haven't walked in our shoes; we, haven't walked in theirs. It's understandable; we have a subjective and somewhat limited ability to give each other what we need. Personal life experiences bias views and shorten attention spans for other peoples' concerns. When you're on the receiving end, it feels unsympathetic. Sometimes, there is no miracle response to our wordy troubles in life. At times, there is only an empathetic smile and a friendly nod of the head. I'm fortunate to have had some good friends who tried to understand me and listened when they could easily say, "Enough already." They've given me the incredible gift of time, allowing me to find what is needed without judgment. And over time, it became increasingly apparent. To expect every friend to support and advise on demand was inappropriate and potentially damaging.

I was walking with a neighbor decades ago, and unfortunately for both of us, was deeply immersed in my complaining years. This day was like many others as I dominated the conversation, ranting about the unfairness of life. Only on this day, she snapped back, severely and harshly, giving me cause to reflect. No one, including myself, has the right to demand support. I ultimately learned to ask myself questions honestly and with self-compassion. After all, no one knows my experiences or the subsequent and complex reactions better than I do. After assessing where I felt wronged, justified or not, my path, including the missteps, was more easily understood and ultimately embraced.

In reviewing my unfortunate actions to different trials, I've experienced "scream in the pillow" moments. Yet, I was ultimately able to say, "It's no surprise I reacted like that." My experiences and responses had a purpose, and that purpose nurtured perseverance, mended character, and gave hope.

> Romans 5:3-4 "Not only so, but we also glory in our sufferings, because we know that suffering produces perseverance; perseverance, character; and character, hope."

thirteen

Broken Becomes Whole

Respite is insight sleeping in the soul
Awakened by the unsettled being
With flawless timing, broken becomes whole

Where's my will to pass the lure of a hole?
Does recurrence find answers farseeing?
Respite is insight sleeping in the soul

Why must I suffer by losing control?
To hold onto the will to start seeing?
With flawless timing, broken becomes whole

What appeared an irreversible toll
My self-worth will begin overseeing
Respite is insight sleeping in the soul

Embracing acceptance helps to console
And begins to awaken wellbeing
With flawless timing, broken becomes whole

To calmly embrace the ultimate goal
That all things are intended is freeing
Respite is insight sleeping in the soul
With flawless timing, broken becomes whole

*To calmly embrace the ultimate goal
That all things are intended is freeing ~*

A close friend once said, "I feel sorry for people who *haven't* had a rough road. They don't know how good it feels to come through on the other side." Her insight framed negative experiences and emotions as unexpected gifts rather than unending self-punishment.

Learning techniques to find calm after chaos comes with time. For me, it's utilizing sage expressions from others. After reading a quote from actress Carrie Fisher that in part read, "Find heaven by backing away from hell," I need only use two of her words to reset myself when moving in the wrong direction of negative thinking, "back away…back away." The relief is immediate. Though tending to distance myself from people in general, I embrace having something in common with them through validating situations and feelings put into words. Sage words are shockingly calming and come to us with flawless timing. My hat is off to you, Carrie Fisher, and anyone sharing honest stories, struggles, and favorable resolutions. Charles Dickens said "No one is useless in this world who lightens the burdens of another." Shared words that ease suffering absolutely lighten the burdens of others.

> "I heard someone say once that many of us only seem able to find heaven by backing away from hell.
> And while the place that I've arrived at in my life may not precisely be everyone's idea of heavenly, I could swear sometimes, I hear angels sing." – Carrie Fisher

fourteen

Valuable

*You see a worthless girl who's wild
I see a lost and broken child
Needing protection, craving direction
Falling victim to those who smiled*

*Easy prey for those who self-serve
Wrongly thinking nothing's left to preserve
Value denied then cast aside
Naïve to the self-worth we deserve*

*Learning to forgive our past and mistakes
Knowing we're worth the effort it takes
To build self-compassion brick by brick
At long last a sense of worth awakes*

*Even amongst seemingly unfavorable,
hostile ground, a flower can grow ~*

Aging has brought the gift of losing a youthful but vulnerable exterior. It's also given me insight from my own journey, coupled with the validating walks of others gracious enough to share their stories. Regarding the following quote by Queen Latifah, I, too, wish those days would come back, at least in regard to dignity and expectations.

> "If women would stop giving up their bodies so quick, it might bring us back to the times when a man would earn a woman's affection. I wish those days would come back. Women felt special, and men stepped up to the plate and showed their dignity."
> - Queen Latifah (from her book *Ladies First*)

In the movie *The Quiet Man*, Sean Thorton (John Wayne) courts Mary Kate Danaher (Maureen O'Hara) while being chaperoned by the town matchmaker/bookie Michaeleen Oge Flynn. Before boarding a one-horse jaunting car (passengers sit back-to-back on a horse-drawn carriage) driven by Mr. Flynn, they're given instructions for a proper courting session. This takes place *after* having been permitted to court in the first place, permission granted by Mary Kate's brother, Will.

Will: "I'm permitting this man to court me sister, but under the usual conditions. Mr. Flynn, do you assume the full responsibility?"

Mr. Flynn: "I do, I do. And from now on, they do the walking and the talking under me own eyes."

Will: "Well then, let the courting commence."

As Sean attempts to assist Mary Kate onto the carriage, he is immediately stopped by Mr. Flynn ~

Mr. Flynn: "Hey, none of that now, none of that, hands to yourself on your own side of the road. Get on the other side of the car."

Sean and Mary Kate take their positions on the carriage, with their backs facing one another. The carriage departs from a crowd of townspeople who are hooting and hollering in excitement.

Was the movie scene idealized? Perhaps, but it likely captures, in part, the intentions and attitudes of the time. Even with those views in place, did improper behaviors still happen? Of course. But I'd rather live with the expectations and hope for more dignified behavior than no expectations and little hope for it.

But that was then, and this is now. While taking very short hikes in Dinosaur National Park on the border of Colorado and Utah, I was stopped in my tracks. The ground was hard and dry, mostly barren and speckled with small rock pebbles. Visible chaos had taken place over the years, including uplifted rock formations that were foreboding, yet, beautiful in a humbling way. Amongst it all were delicate flowers growing in that hard, dry soil. Even amongst seemingly unfavorable, hostile ground, a flower can grow.

Fifteen

The Fifth Season

The springtime of my teenage years, would not ever, know the fall
For summer came and went so fast, that winter, would end it all
And right before that cold winter came, fifth season flickered by
And snatched with a selfish secrecy, fall, and the answers why

Why does fifth season pick and choose, for whom, it carries its scythe
Why take my father, season of fall, and good intent in life
For before my father passed away, I gambled time was there
Time for me to find my way, so I could properly repair

The growing pains that hindered me, it's a weight I now endure
I feel like he's a stranger now, and I wait for time to cure
Somewhere in that unwelcome season, conversations have stood
Lying dormant with understanding, and resolved childhood

Until I can forgive myself, and cleanse embedded regrets
I believe I'll know my father when compassion then resets
Beneath a wing of empathy, self-reproach will find self-care
And then I feel my father, will help me shed the load I bear

*Why does fifth season pick and choose,
for whom, it carries its scythe ~*

My father was taken from this place when I was nineteen years old. Like many young people, I was troubled and needed time to sort through life. Time was not on my side. Things were said that couldn't be unsaid. Maturing changed from the standard way to the hard knocks' way, and recognizing who was there to help, and, more importantly, who was there to harm.

Coming to terms with a past that could not be changed had only one option. That option is an opportunity to find purpose and comfort in why things happened the way they did. I've matured slowly, but perhaps "deeper" than someone having the cocoon of both parents for a good deal of their life. My belief is that my father would be proud of who I am today, giving me a dose of parental love even though he's not here. He is a part of something I will eventually be a part of, entirely and mercifully. Knowing what I've overcome and recognizing who I do not want to be may not have happened any other way.

> "You may delay, but time will not."
> - Benjamin Franklin

PART IV
Acceptance

sixteen

Unforgiven

Acknowledged mistake, apology given
Ill-fated response, unforgiven
An added punishment
To a lapse in judgement
Mercy can be given but not taken

Though I've offered various and sincere apologies over a lifetime, I've offered them at least twice for which I've been genuinely denied forgiveness. I don't know that there's a greater punishment to inflict than denying forgiveness. My apologies don't come easily; if I apologize for something, I genuinely feel bad about doing it. So, when it became clear my words would not be embraced, it was a sickening feeling. Life experiences bias everything, especially expectations of people. Where one person might reject an apology for a specific incident, another might warmly embrace the same request. My offenses and subsequent discarded apologies produced tough lessons in reflection, learning to let go, and ultimately, acceptance.

A rejected apology is an isolating feeling and feels personal. It's a harsh termination of outside approval for an apology. Once again, the welcome words from others have helped. The Greek philosopher Epictetus said, "If you are ever tempted to look for outside approval, realize that you have compromised your integrity. If you need a witness, be your own."

seventeen

From this Day Forward

*It feels not all that long ago
We seemed the perfect pair
But dreams began to fall away
And took commitment there*

*To love and to cherish, to have and to hold
You promised me you would
But now I have to move along
I never thought I could*

*From this day forward now has new meaning
One I will accept
But in my heart I know I'm worthy
A conviction I have kept*

*Contentment, calm and happiness
Are gifts I have again
For after all, God has a plan
And I choose to trust in Him*

I was in my early twenties when a friend a few years older, yet already in a failing marriage, said, "Marriage is the hardest thing you'll ever do." I was young and single and couldn't relate. Worse yet, her heartfelt comment seemed uninteresting and was tucked away with little thought.

Years later, after witnessing the progression of events that led to the breakdowns of several friends' marriages, often taking decades, her words revealed much truth. In addition, I had my own marital hill to climb. Indeed, it takes ongoing and often ~ agonizing work. The most profound dose of wisdom I've been given regarding ANY relationship came 30 years into my marriage. It was from a friend who said, "In marriage, you have to accept that you may not be able to give each other what you want." It removed the burden of expecting perfection, be it marriage or friendship. Some relationships need to end, but for others, I've little doubt we're meant to adopt a sort of "choose your battles wisely" mindset. I love the following quote by Michael J. Fox; because when it comes to any relationship, it's a form of self-care to lessen expectations.

> "My happiness grows in direct proportion to my acceptance, and in inverse proportion to my expectations."
> - Michael J. Fox, activist and actor

eighteen

The Whisper

*I saw them whisper and point with a nod
I knew it was me, I knew I was flawed
New realization, clear confirmation
What I thought was friendship was fraud*

*I saw them whisper; I wish I hadn't
The closeness I wished to have, I couldn't
Unmistakable, undeniable
The connection I sought they didn't*

*Seeing rejection by way of a glance
A jeering look and judgmental stance
Cannot dismiss the actions remiss
The whisper I saw by chance*

I'm a hypocrite; most of us are. I wouldn't call myself a chronic gossiper, but on occasion I've certainly talked about people behind their backs. It's human nature to want to be heard; nothing perks people's interest like dirt on someone else. It could be we fill empty conversations and proceed in a lazy and flawed fashion. I know because I was one of them, and would often think to myself afterward, "You need to stop." One fateful day, the table was turned ~ in a church parking lot of all places. I was clearly the target of old high school "friends" talking about me. In a three-second display, our eyes locked at the moment they were looking on, as one "pointed" with a nod of the head, and laughter ensued in painful tandem with a muted conversation. It was hurtful but humbling. On one hand, I knew, like a slap in the face, exactly what my worth was to them. On the other hand, it taught me an overdue lesson. This person I childishly wanted the approval of made it brutally apparent there was no need to bother. I'd be a better person for it, but felt the proverbial dunce cap upon my head at that moment. I felt alone, unwanted, and stupid.

A favorite line(s) from the movie *My Cousin Vinny* happens in a bar when Vinny (Joe Pesci) tries to collect money on behalf of his girlfriend Lisa (Marisa Tomei), who won a bet from a fellow bar patron. When the fellow patron refuses to pay but instead threatens to fight Vinny, Vinny responds as though it's a choice. He says, "Hmm, what should I do? Get my ass kicked or collect $200? I could use a good ass kicking; I'm not gonna lie."

I'm not going to lie, either. I needed a humility kick, and I got one. Though the scene with Joe Pesci was comical, and my personal experience was anything but, it did validate one thing. We have skeletons in our closets, we're far from perfect, and the table will turn from time to time. But with that in-your-face lesson came a good dose of wisdom and a necessary measure of humility from an unlikely messenger.

> "Don't speak evil of someone if you don't know for certain, and if you do know ask yourself,
> why am I telling it?"
> -Johann Kaspar Lavater, poet

nineteen

Surrendering

*Born into life with a predisposition
Losing control, a painful admission
Fueled by environment
Yet needing self-discipline
Ask God for relief, must humbly give in*

*A life out of hand, only He can wield
Honesty, faith, and work form a shield
A predisposition
A frightful condition
Surrendering to God can heal*

A life out of hand, only He can wield ~

At age 58, well-immersed on a journey of self-discipline, or so I thought, and holding my proverbial sobriety token, BOOM, off the wagon I fell. My temper flared, this time with a total stranger. The excuses were all there. Having recently been diagnosed with cancer, both surgery and subsequent treatments were on the docket. My son's wedding was weeks away, and the ensuing classic family drama had been activated. Lastly, a very close relationship had recently soured, ruffling my feathers. Though the recipient of my anger was perhaps less than happy with her job at that particular business, she didn't deserve my outburst. I was truly ready to have God remove my defects of character" *(Step 6 of the 12-step recovery program).*

Alcoholics Anonymous, undoubtedly the most recognized of the 12-step recovery programs, addresses a fundamental principle: we are powerless over genetic and environmental disadvantages, but we are not powerless over our responses to them. Ironically (or not), the book for another 12-step program, *Overeaters Anonymous*, fell into my lap like so many other books have; sometimes God seems so obvious! As I paged through the steps, I saw their fluidity as they pertain to so many challenging aspects of life. It's no wonder the rules are universal for the various programs. A brief online search yielded 80 assorted 12-step groups, pretty specific ones. After reading through my 12-step book, I was stopped in my tracks and thought to myself, "What's all this religious stuff doing in here?" The answer was clear. We are tiny in the grand scheme of things and need something bigger than us.

The primary 12 steps, as taken verbatim from *The Twelve Steps and Twelve Traditions of Overeaters Anonymous* book, 2012 edition (though any 12-step program would do), are as follows. Keep in mind how they truly apply to most any problem:

Step One is the admission that "Our lives have become unmanageable."

Step Two, "A Power greater than ourselves could restore us to sanity."

Step Three, "Turn our will and our lives over to the care of God as we understood Him."

Step Four, "Make a searching and fearless moral inventory of ourselves."

Step Five, "Admitted to God, to ourselves, and to another human being the exact nature of our wrongs."

Step Six, "We're entirely ready to have God remove all these defects of character."

Step Seven, "Humbly asked Him to remove our shortcomings."

Step Eight, "Made a list of all persons we had harmed and became willing to make amends to them all."

Step Nine, "Made direct amends to such people wherever possible, except when to do so would injure them or others."

Step Ten, "Continued to take personal inventory and when we were wrong, promptly admitted it."

Step Eleven, "Sought through prayer and meditation to improve our conscious contact with God as we understood Him, praying only for knowledge of His will for us and the power to carry that out."

Step Twelve, "Having had a spiritual awakening as the result of these steps, we tried to carry this message - and to practice these principles in all our affairs."

Be it Alcoholics Anonymous, Emotions, Gambling, Overeaters, and so forth, it doesn't matter. Honesty, faith, and work form a shield.

> "We accept that each defect, as painful to us as it may be, is a part of who we are. With humble acceptance we can quietly say to our Higher Power, 'I am this way, and only with your help can I change.'"
> -The Twelve Steps and Twelve Traditions of OA 2012

twenty

Destiny's Light

Destiny had placed my light
Amongst the glowing stars
And in the dark we'd beam and wink
As providence was ours

But the star that shown the brightest
Drew me closer for a look
I left the safety of my niche
Taking what I should not have took

Like Icarus I flew too close
In search of something when
All along He had me where
I knew I should have been

Unexceptional to the rest
Though perfectly placed, so I
Settled into my celestial bed
No longer self-abased

In Greek mythology, Icarus and his father, Daedalus, used wings fashioned from feathers, leather, and beeswax to escape imprisonment by their king, Minos, on the island of Crete. Despite warnings from his father to fly neither too close to the water nor too close to the sun, Icarus let discontentment get the best of him; he flew too high. The beeswax melts, the wings crumble, and Icarus falls to the ocean below, where he drowns. The story highlights what can happen when we overreach with dissatisfaction.

It wasn't my fate to have a large extended family, though I longed for the idealized John Boy Walton experience. I've envied, often with resentment, those so fortunate. With a "grass is greener" determination, I joined in and lingered in places where I did not fit in. Singer and songwriter Tom Petty said, "You belong somewhere you feel free." During my search, the freedom wasn't there, in my mind, to be myself. Instead, attempting to morph into a sociable person was exactly opposite my nature. Predictably, the genuine awkward self was revealed and I'd either remove myself, or worse, stop receiving invites. I flew too close to the sun. My quest lasted four decades until the realization hit: I *was* where I belonged. I learned that we're not all meant to be the same. Be yourself; accept your lot in life. It sounded defeatist until finding a quote from lifengoal.com, "Accepting your lot in life isn't waving a white flag of surrender; it's about embracing the hand you've been dealt with grace."

PART V
gratitude

twenty-one

A Valued Friendship

*I learned to value friendship
When a close friend chose to stay
After having seen the faults in me
Solid ground won't break away*

*My friend embraced our differences
Knowing when to give me space
There never was a scorecard
Condemnation had no place*

*Trying to fit in
While in unison, trying to hide
So few can accept, or understand
But my friend stood by my side*

*My hat is off to you, my friend
For this life has brought me few
Of the unconditional sort of heart
The kind inside of you*

Wayne Dyer, author and motivational speaker, said, "Happiness is easy, but learning not to be unhappy can be difficult." Indeed, it can. After a close friendship fell apart, I was hurt, really hurt, and my fallback defense mechanism was anger.

Writing *A Valued Friendship* began with pain at the core, and so commenced, "I learned to value friendship when a close friend walked away." Beyond that, my intent was to reflect and expand on the hurt and subsequent anger. Then Wayne Dyers' words awakened me: Learn not to be unhappy. After all, I had several good friends who were aware of any shortcomings I possessed, yet chose to stay with the help of honest conversations. There are very genuine reasons to learn not to be unhappy.

> "Close friends are truly life's treasures. Sometimes they know us better than we know ourselves."
> - Vincent van Gogh

twenty-two

A Charming Ol' Gal

She straightened her frame, postured for the sale
A striking round door, brass slot for the mail
She squeaked with joy as we walked down her halls
Held her head high within old plaster walls

She beckoned us up the staircase with soft,
Well-worn wood rails, to a redesigned loft
Windows exhibited stained glass with pride
Strutting her stuff from both out and inside

Well-used stone base, a bit worn, truth be told
It's lasted this long, she's not all that old
Her jobs been done well, with love, from the past
New homes can't compare, her charm's unsurpassed

When my son and daughter-in-law went house hunting for their first home and wanted an older home near St. Louis, they were in for the debate of their lives. Most homes were right at or nearing one hundred years old; they reeked of both character and legitimate concerns. Working with a respectable but not an unlimited budget, future unanticipated repairs and marital stress were genuinely authentic. Have you seen the movie *The Money Pit?*

My husband and I were all too familiar with owning and renovating an older home after having gutted our first one, a 90-year-old frame house, down to the stud walls. Having had the experience was good, but ignorance was no longer bliss. We knew what lay hidden behind the fetching and unique character traits. Blemished foundations, knob-and-tube wiring, dated plumbing, root-infested utility service lines, leaky windows, plaster, and its Siamese twin, plaster lath, are but a few of the challenges. But the beauty and character of an older home are irreplaceable; newer homes lack character and are predictable and overly safe. Gone are the pocket doors, clawfoot tubs, laundry chutes, telephone alcoves, stained glass windows, and arched doorways. Saving the older "ladies" of architecture is a worthy cause. They possess a maternal quality and deserve more than a wrecking ball. They're clear reminders of how meticulous craftsmanship and pride in ownership were, and still can be.

twenty-three

Time Well-Served

She pranced close to my side for a lifetime
In the beginning she pulled firm ahead
But as the years went by, long past her prime
The reality of time went unsaid

It's painful to watch a soul that you love
Wear a timepiece that goes by much quicker
Than the struggling sort, unworthy of
Loyalty that goes by in a flicker

Just like a flower highlighting its dew
It's beauty and gifts are short-lived, as for
Time is certainty the clock will accrue
But a memory, tenderly relived

Our four-legged friends are gifts undeserved
A gift of perfection, and time well-served

*Just like a flower highlighting its dew
It's beauty and gifts are short-lived ~*

While walking with my aging dog, I noticed and photographed dew-covered flowers. It was yet another gift from my four-legged friend that was, quite possibly, spiritually deliberate. We're bombarded with what we should be aware of daily. It seems we need a lot of help, and God and His universe can get creative.

So, on that day and during our walk, her pace had slowed as it had been for some time. Compelled to either daydream, get frustrated, or take careful note of my beautiful surroundings, the flowers nearly reached out to me while pausing with my faithful friend. This precious soul that walked by my side and was once full of almost unmanageable robust energy was now experiencing the effects of aging. Though it's painful to watch a loved one age, there was beauty in witnessing her gracefully going through the stages, wagging her tail through it all. It was humbling, and I knew, "I'm so undeserving of this friendship.

Indeed, she and they are in this place for a much shorter time. They come here having already mastered loyalty and unconditional affection. I've long believed that our purpose "here" is to learn; they may be here to help teach.

> "All his life he tried to be a good person.
> Many times, however, he failed.
> For after all, he was only human.
> He wasn't a dog." - Charles M. Schulz

twenty-four

Tom

*The smallest of small businesses
Was the cheeriest of all
And occupied the living room
Where Tom lived, down the hall*

*It was in the yellow bungalow
built in 1936
That a mom did what a mom would do
And fixed what needed fixed*

*She emptied out the living room
And replaced the couch with shelves
And filled the room with retail goods
So they could work the store themselves*

*Not least of all, Tom in his wheelchair
Wearing kindness upon his face
Taking what Polio could not take
Making the best of life, with grace*

Memories from childhood and their lasting feelings stand out from that child's perspective. After taking note of the slightly unusual setting of a small neighborhood store, I quickly accepted it as "very cool" and the norm. Located in an ordinary middle-class neighborhood in the mid-seventies, the store was quite literally in someone's (Tom's) living room. The 964-sf little yellow home, small by today's standards, had been repurposed to utilize the entire living room as a working grocery store, complete with small aisles, staple foods, refrigerated items, and a fantastic candy counter. In the front yard was a small yellow sign planted in the ground, "Tom's Grocery." Tom, who was confined to a wheelchair, ran the store alongside his mother. She assisted in the operation until her passing when Tom subsequently took the reins. Conveniently located between my grade school and home, I often stopped to purchase jumbo-sized Pixy Stix and Hershey chocolate bars (10 cents each) along with Pez candy at a mere 2 cents a pack. And Tom was unfailingly smiling, embodying kindness. The local mailman was often present, talking and laughing alongside Tom, creating an atmosphere likened to Mr. Rogers's Neighborhood. Poet and playwright Oscar Wilde once said, "Memory is the diary that we all carry about with us." Tom's Grocery is one of those fond entries in my childhood diary of memories.

twenty-five

A Lifted Soul

Poetry lifts the soul and floats beyond
Where continuous thoughts lie still below
And passionate feelings are briefly calmed

From benevolent words waiting to bond
To fragmented spirits of those who know
Poetry lifts the soul and floats beyond

Verses search, little ripples in a pond
To stir life's unrelenting drumbeat so
The passionate feelings are briefly calmed

Poems wait with compassion to respond
To needs from parallel hardships and show
Poetry lifts the soul and floats beyond

An immortal method to correspond
Seeds in the ground at the proper time grow
And passionate feelings are briefly calmed

A quatrain of words or sonnet will find
Its way through fate and destiny to glow
Poetry lifts the soul and floats beyond
And passionate feelings are briefly calmed

Poetry lifts the soul and floats beyond

I didn't connect to poetry growing up. According to the internet that puts me in the roughly 90 percent of the population who don't, or did not regularly read it. Nevertheless, my lifestyle eventually gravitated toward reading and writing it. As I write, some poems come to me effortlessly, as in writing *This Fellow Man, Lone Goose* and *Time Well-Served*, almost like they were already there, as George Michael puts it ~

> "When I write a lyric in my head, something at the back of my neck just knows that I've hit it. It's almost like it was already there, but you hadn't spotted where it was yet. It's almost like it comes to you fully formed, and you just pulled it out of nowhere, and the feeling that you have that makes you shiver, is that, you found it."
> - George Michael (2024 Netflix Doc *Wham*)

Other poems are more like journaling in that they try to make sense of things. *A Lifted Soul*, written in the poetry structure of a Villanelle, journals the reprieve that both reading and writing poetry can offer. Many thoughts that ramble through our heads can be comforting, much like backseat driving*, as mentioned in the prologue for Part VI. But occasionally it's good to have a break from all the noise below, and still the continuous thoughts in our heads.

PART VI
humor

In the book *The Untethered Soul* by Michael A. Singer, the author states (about the voice inside your head), "The narration makes you feel more comfortable with the world around you. *Like backseat driving, it makes you feel as though things are more in your control." Writing is my "backseat driving," reflecting that which consumes my thoughts. Writing verbalizes the obstacles in life, the struggle to overcome them, and the necessary humor that balances it all. Thus, I finish with the humorous side of things: the lifesaving buoy ring amidst an abyss of water. The first three poems and ensuing stories address the discomfort of different situations, along with the blessings of humor in hindsight. The last two stories are from my second book, *Adventures with Ruby Slippers*, to once more share the comedy in that which makes us perfectly human: our imperfections.

> "Humor is just another
> defense against the universe."
> - Mel Brooks

twenty-six

May-September

A gal who was just beyond twenty
Refuted a man older by plenty
And she didn't refrain
As she began to explain
To a woman, years older than she

The older gal sat back and listened
With a smirk and eyes that glistened
Of the man who took a chance
On a May-September romance
And the gal who would tell but not kiss and

In my early twenties, I found myself in an embarrassing situation after being asked on a date by a man who was at least 30 years my senior. Now, there are two ways of looking at that scenario. There's the scrunched-up face reaction, or the "weird, but kind of funny!" reaction. I chose the latter, especially when the entire story played out in all its glory. Because despite our faults, or perhaps because of them, humans really can be funny.

"The situation" began while I was a part of a local bicycle club that cycled several times a week. We were a healthy group, in more ways than one, and cycled anywhere from 25-100 miles on our rides. Group members ranged from 20 years of age to around 70. One warm summer day, having just stopped for a water break at a four-way stop in the middle of nowhere, "Frank" and I were temporarily separated from the group. Frank found this opportune, catching me completely off-guard with a bold question, leaving me temporarily speechless:

Frank: Carol, I know I'm too old to be romantic, but would you like to go to dinner sometime?

Me: (long pause) I'm sorry (another long pause). My boyfriend wouldn't like that too much.

Though Frank dropped the subject, his attempt at wooing played out on another ride and a different day. But before that humorous interaction, I sat down with another club member, "Barb," who was in the 50-60-year-old range, like Frank. I unburdened myself of the story while she listened with a smirk and wide eyes, ending with robust laughter.

The cat was out of the bag as Barb and I peddled together on a group ride later that summer. On that day, temperatures bordered on uncomfortably cool, but like most bikers who count on warming up as the day progresses, we BOTH donned only bike shorts and t-shirts. My knight in shining armor came to my rescue, catching up and peddling alongside long enough to deliver another passive-aggressive reminder of his availability.

Frank: Carol, it's kind of chilly, would you like to wear my jacket?

Me: No, I think I'm good, but thanks anyway!

And off he peddles, leaving my much older but far closer to his age riding partner, also wearing shorts and a t-shirt, in the lurch. Frank, ignorantly bliss that I'd spilled the beans weeks prior, peddled away and out of earshot as Barb's grin widened. She responded humorously to Franks's careless, if not egotistical, display while purposely donning a shaky old woman's voice, "Us old women get cold too, Frank..." We both bust out laughing and continued on our ride. She was, without a doubt, a very positive and aging-with-grace woman; someone to look up to. It was a good day.

> "Beautiful young people are accidents of nature,
> but beautiful old people are works of art."
> - Eleanor Roosevelt

twenty-seven

A Gifted Memory

*The curse of poor recollection
Gives way to quite a collection
Of cringe-worthy moments
Ironic bestowments, of an
unforgettable memory selection*

I can't remember what I had for lunch, I can't remember the name of a person who introduced themselves literally five minutes ago, but I sure can remember "deer in the headlight" moments when my brain burned a new, cringe-worthy memory in the place of the forgotten one. The following story is from my first book *Adventures in Small Business*, and details the unfortunate ramifications of a poor memory, especially in an environment where you really should remember names, faces, and stories.

In working with customers (in a small retail store) whose paths crossed mine sometimes once, sometimes only a handful of times, there really weren't any consequences to brutal honesty on their part. Because of this, my flaws were pointed out on occasion, in cold-blood. I fully admit that I have no gift for remembering names, faces, and details, which can be a real problem. Recalling my bosses' words at an old job drives home not only how poor my memory can be, but that it's no secret; he reminded me in a non-nonsense way. When a coworker asked me for more information on a job site we worked on the previous day, my boss couldn't chime in quick enough. He hollered from across the very small work space, "What the F*$K are you asking her for? She can't f*$king remember what she had for lunch today." Although I believe he was fond enough of me (yes, I'm serious), he didn't mince words, not at all. Plus, he liked to use the F word, a lot.

Fast forward to a day at the store when my curse reared its head high after hearing some very cringe-worthy words…

On this day, my attempt at trying to be a warm and welcoming store owner backfired. My brain, in particular the section for memory, was only partially functioning, as usual. A female customer was browsing the store, making light conversation during which she mentioned her profession as a home health care nurse visiting from another state. She alternates spending two weeks here then returns home for the other two weeks, some five or six hours away. Finding this fascinating, I raised my eyebrows and genuinely said with some excitement, "OH REALLY?!" She gave me the "You're truly are a moron" look, and then she said, "Yeah, and we go through this EVERY TIME I'M HERE."

I stood frozen for a second, processing a reply in which there is no good reply, shrunk several inches, and smiled one doofus of a smile as my tail curled in-between my legs. After delivering my weak apology and repeating to myself, "For crying out loud, remember her face, remember her face!" I murmured a reply. My pathetic response was, "Well, I guess I'll remember you now." Boy, I hope I remember her next time. I take that back, if there's one face that's burned into my mind, it's hers. The memory, is a funny thing. Hardy, har, har.

twenty-eight

Growing Pains

A middle school misfortune
Got blown out of proportion, when
A gal threw a ball
That would tragically fall
On the head of a thug, but then ~

The tragedy lies in the verdict
Delivered where it most would hurt it
A swift kick in the _ss
In the shower after class
With clothes on she would've preferred it

Middle school is a rite of passage. Memories of harsh realities can be funny, but I wasn't laughing then. In our town of 25,000, several elementary schools merged into one large middle school, where you're either a bully, or not, and I was not. Having been all but bubble-wrapped in elementary school, I was in for a wake-up call.

While playing basketball in gym class, I threw the ball at the hoop and made a perfect shot, that is, until it swished through the net and landed on the head of a school bully. As if it were my fault, she gave me the stink-eye while pondering my sentence. It would be mercilessly delivered in the locker room, specifically, the shower room. While buck naked (both of us), she approached me from behind and gave me a swift kick in the butt. I guess on a positive note, it was over with just like that, but wow. ☹

The locker room was a vulnerable place, as was the school bus ride home. One ill-fated day, I boarded the bus and searched for an empty seat for my friend and myself. Bus protocol was understood. Bullies took the rear, and the safer, but nearly impossible-to-get seats, were near the front. Seat selection depended entirely on the location of your last class. As misfortune would have it, my last class was an outlier, making it impossible to secure a seat near the front. Making my way down the aisle, I found and sat on the first available bench seat, in the rear. Unbeknownst to me, that seat was earmarked for a particular bully, who arrived shortly afterward. She told me to move, to which I politely responded with my need to save the seat for my friend. Again, justice would be swift.

She yelled out to the nearly full bus, "What stop does this chick get off at?!" The crowds cheerfully resounded in unison, "Bus stop #3!!" It was my rare moment of popularity. My friend sat with me silently as I pondered the limited options: fight or flight. Flight seemed reasonable, and as the bus rolled to a stop, I strolled to the front along with spectators and the bully on my tail. Then, picking up my pace down the steps, I pounced on the ground and sprinted while doing a quick scan of the horizon. I zeroed in on an elderly gentleman tending his garden, racing to his side as my emotions burst. The cheetah retreated, I got back my breath, then spilled my story. This grandfatherly soul then served up some shocking advice, "why didn't you just hit her?!" I mumbled, "She would've beat me up." He summed up his personal philosophy bluntly, "Well, at least you would've gotten one good hit in." I don't think his strategy would've ended well for me.

On a lighter note, disco dancing in seventh-grade gym class, though nightmarish for shy kids, had to have been funny for onlookers. Graded on participation, I had little choice, so I slipped into a disassociated state and went to town. But then, I looked over to see my friend fixated on me, laughing. After having been clearly caught, she apologized (sort of) by saying, "I'm sorry, but you just looked so funny!" Rite of passage.

> "You can't be brave if you've only had wonderful things happen to you." - Mary Tyler Moore, Actress

twenty-nine

Chickens and Roosters

There once was a gal with grey hair
Who enticed the old men to stare
The chickens began to cluck
When the roosters ran amuck
Falling victim to an eye candy snare

What do you do if you have an RV and are semi-retired? The next logical step: buy an outrageous amount of outdoor furniture and décor, cram it in your RV, and find out what this snowbird thing is all about. So, we head South, to Florida, like grey-haired metal to a magnet. When we found the stereotypes were true, it was jarring, but funny. It was a mixture of chuckling and hackles standing up on our backs, pondering if we were truly ready to be a part of the snowbird community. After all, funny can only calm so many concerns.

And concerning it was, from witnessing the daily parade of battery-assisted bicycle rides to finding yourself looking forward to the weekly calendar of events, the same calendar we found silly at the start. Though we weren't really ready to join in the festivities, and weren't sure we'd ever be, it highlighted the relevance of a cringe-worthy statement from an RV park owner. She responded to our request to book one of her better spots for the following year and said, "they're all booked right now, but you can put your name on the waitlist. With the age group we're dealing with, there are a lot of cancellations if you know what I mean." Wow, yeah, I do know what you mean.

Reluctantly accepting that we were technically entering into an older faction of society, it was time to find out if it was true that old people, in general, get nicer as they age. Now, I can only speak for women, and while I'll say in general, they do, they *never* entirely lose that catty attitude. Thus, I share my accounting of chickens and roosters.

After checking into an RV park in Florida during snowbird season, we were handed a monthly calendar of events. Organized activities are the hallmark of any good RV park versus the subpar. However hokey, it adds to the overall funny flavor of, "wow, this is so, so weird." On the other hand, I have to admit that my eagerness to look at the calendar was troubling. I went down a dark road and began marking the calendar with stars and smiley faces. Bingo nights including free popcorn and participants who took the whole thing way too seriously took priority, while cornhole tournaments, trivia nights, aqua-aerobics, and pancake breakfasts, all part of the overall vibe, added a charming flair. On this particular day, the much-anticipated cornhole tournament was on the docket, and men and women alike had circled their camping chairs like wild west wagons. One lady, probably at retirement age or slightly older, decided to wear a bikini and do several laps around the wagons, including numerous older men who happily peered on. Their better halves were less than pleased. For her age, she looked damned good; shoot, she looked great for most anyone half her age. My high school years lit up briefly when the hens began clucking at the clear and present danger. Yup, women don't change much, even as they get older. But in all fairness, neither do men.

> "Here's all you have to know about men and women: women are crazy, men are stupid. And the main reason women are crazy is that men are stupid."
> - George Carlin

thirty

Splendor

*There was a young lady of tender
good looks, refinement and splendor
But she let out a toot
Like an underwater flute
And froze as if all eyes were on her*

During a family camping trip at an RV campground in Canada, my husband and I bore witness to a regrettably relatable scene from a fellow camperette who learned an innocent lesson the humble way. Years after the fact, we still chuckle at the incident that took place at the campground park pool. All we have to do is look at each other and make the most minor verbal fart noise, and we both smile, shake our heads and chuckle. The scene took place after arriving at the campground pool; our two young sons swam nearby as we sat poolside with our legs dangling in the water. A young lady, probably about 18 years old, was sitting on the opposite edge of the pool. She was, by all standards, delicate as she was pretty. She, too, had her legs dangling in the water, enjoying her last few moments of splendor. It was then that the unthinkable happened. In the moment's calm, we heard a not-so-small fart while we were simultaneously, and unfortunately for her, looking in her direction. Then, a look of absolute horror washed over her pretty little face as her not-so-silent fart had come out with a comical sound. She badly underestimated the wet bikini bottom effect of trying to "let one escape." We wanted to help her save face as we neither laughed nor hinted that we heard her cute little fart. She was caught between a rock and a hard place; get up and gather her pride, or carry on? She sat there frozen; the poor thing really was mortified.

> "Pride divides the men, humility joins them."
> -Socrates

Epilogue

I've learned I cannot be perfect
~ a lesson that gifted *humility* and *empathy*

I've learned to reasonably guard candor
~ a lesson that gifted *protection* from reproach

I've learned those closest to you will hurt you most
~ a lesson that gifted *calm* through lowering expectations

I've learned to embrace my need for occasional solitude
~ a lesson that gifted *peace* through embracing my needs

I've learned it's abusive to perpetually complain to others
~ a lesson that gifted *resolution*, opting to look inward

I've learned that a tiny dose of selfishness can be healthy
~ a lesson that gifted *permission* to caringly guard myself

I've learned that I cannot change the people around me
~ a lesson that gifted *relief* from the burden of conflict

I've learned humor usually outweighs negativity
~ gifting some *freedom* from the weight of a world

about the author

Carol McManus shares both light-hearted and solemn poetry from teachable moments and the gifts they bring. *The Tree on the Bluff* follows *Adventures with Ruby Slippers* and her first book, *Adventures in Small Business*, both steeped in the lively energy surrounding us. After toggling between Illinois, Virginia, Washington, and Missouri, she settled in Missouri with her family. Amongst the moves in many towns and on many streets was a small cedar-sided home on a picturesque pine tree-laden street named Kipling Way. The street name sparked an interest in the poet Rudyard Kipling and subsequent poetry by various authors; another demonstration of how the universe delivers what you need, when you need it. Thus, Carols' previous indifference to poetry turned to appreciating it and its ability to capture, validate, and release vast feelings.

I hope you enjoyed reading my book as much as I enjoyed writing it! If you liked reading The Tree on the Bluff, I would appreciate it if you shared your experience with an online review. This feedback helps me in addition to future readers. To leave a review on Amazon, simply log in, find my book, scroll down to the bottom of the page and find the reviews, then hit the button that says "Write a customer review." I appreciate your time, thank you so much! - C.L. McManus